D1616463

better together*

*This book is best read together, grownup and kid.

a kids book about™

technology

by Amber Case

a
kids
book
about™

A Kids Book About books are available online:
www.akidsbookabout.com

To share your stories, ask questions, or inquire about bulk
purchases (schools, libraries, and nonprofits), please use
the following email address:

hello@akidsbookabout.com

ISBN: 978-1-951253-83-7

Designed by Duke Stebbins
Edited by Denise Morales Soto

Dedicated to my mom and dad.

And my backyard tree.

Intro

This book is about helping grownups and kids learn about the role technology has in their life and their relationship with it. This is also a book about time. The value and quality of your time, how you can spend it, and about the importance of achieving balance in our lives and with technology.

But remember, technology is everything that we use in the world, from poetry to pottery, from books to your television. So my goal is not to take kids away from technology, but rather help them see the joys and benefits of spending some of their time away from their computers and devices and discover all that life has to offer.

This is a kids book about **technology**.

But this book *isn't* about:

how playing video games is bad,
or how to keep you safe online,
or why you should spend
less time on your phone,
or how to use a computer,
or how to build a computer!

No, this book is about how we feel when we use technology.

But before we can understand that, we need to know—

what is technology?

Sometimes we think technology is just computers, but it's actually **EVERYTHING around you!**

From a seed, to a tree, to a pair of glasses, to this book you're reading now!

A lot of technology works like a tool
that allows us to do something useful
or fun—like a hammer and a phone.

They're both tools!

But while technology is meant to help you, different kinds of technology can affect us differently.

Especially newer technology
like computers, cellphones,
and other devices.

 That's what we're going to be
focusing on today.

You see, I grew up in a
home filled with technology,
so I know a lot about this stuff.

*You could even say it's part of
my genetic code.*

My family members built computers,
synthesizers, microphones,
and speakers.

My aunt made trailers for
Hollywood movies!

My grandfather was even one of the first
people to help build the Internet.
THE INTERNET!

So I grew up building, making, creating, and learning with all kinds of technology.

I played outside with the *first technology:*

nature!

trees!

sticks!

With the technology of the notebook,
I would write and draw and
make my own worlds.

Then I got my first computer
and took my exploring indoors.

To be honest, **I LOVE**

TECHNOLOGY!

But sometimes it can be lonely.

That's the thing about technology, sometimes you use it by yourself.

 Even when you're chatting, talking, or playing with someone else, you can still feel alone.

 Sometimes I would look at what others did online and I felt like I wasn't smart enough.

 Sometimes I saw other people playing and I felt left out.

But other times I would use technology to learn new things and make new friends!

That's the thing with technology, it can feel different depending on how we use it.

Sometimes we use it for fun and to create.

Sometimes we browse through the web even when we know we should be doing something else.

Sometimes we use it to escape.

Sometimes we use it to connect.

Sometimes we use it because we don't feel like there is anything better to do.

Sometimes when we use technology we don't know when to stop!

Technology isn't good or bad.

+500

What makes it good or bad is
how and **_when_** we use it,
and **_what_** we use it for.

Even though the connected technology we use every day is made up of glass, metal, wires, and transistors…

We can get out of balance in how we use it in our lives, and being out of balance affects our bodies and how we feel.

swipe for an example!

<

Have you ever lost track of time while staring at a screen?

 You were doing something then realize, all of a sudden, that you've been staring at your devices for so long that your body has frozen up!

You eventually realize...

🔔 3 notifications

You're hungry.
You're late for something.
You're tired.

Technology can sometimes
be so consuming we forget
all about our bodies!

But your body is a very special thing.

Your body has needs.

your body needs

your body needs **to eat food**

your body needs **to move**

your body needs **a hug**

your body needs **fun!**

No matter how hungry you are, your phone can't feed you a meal, or give you a hug, or make you truly happy.

Our devices and technology seem like they're giving us those things, but in reality, they're not.

They're just substitutes for the real thing.

No matter how much time
you spend sitting with technology,
it won't give your body what
it needs to stay strong.

Your body still needs to walk
around to keep working.

This doesn't make technology bad, we just need to be careful about how we use it.

How we use our technology is connected to how we spend our time.

Do you ever think about time?

The Greeks thought about time **a lot**.

They thought about it **SO MUCH** that they actually had multiple words for it!

I want to teach you those words.

The first word is...

CHRO

Chronos time is when you have something you need to do and have to make sure it gets done.

Like when you have a doctor's appointment or the time you need to be in class.

NOS!

When you spend this kind of time,
you might feel tired afterward,
but you also might feel productive
or accomplished.

The second word is...

Kairos time is quality time. When you spend this kind of time, you might feel refreshed and inspired.

Kairos time is going on a walk, drawing, or showing something we made to our parents or loved ones.

ROS!

Special ability unlocked!

Ancient Greek: level 1

Sometimes we have to spend **Chronos** time doing chores or homework.

When we complete them we feel better afterward, but it can be hard to do!

Kairos time is time we *want* to experience.

Sometimes we might feel guilty when we use our **Kairos** time so it's hard to remember to enjoy it!

You might feel like there is too much to do, or that it's easier to spend time on your devices...

But we all need Kairos time.

Because Kairos time is human time, and we all need that!

Kairos time allows us to dream and imagine.

It reminds us that we're alive.

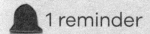

But sometimes we get stuck in looping time.

Sometimes we're upset about
what someone said online
and can't stop thinking about it,

or we sit still for too long
and our body hurts,

or we stare at screens for hours
and our minds feel hazy and tired.

You might be wondering,
how do we get out of times like this?

Times when we aren't feeling so great
or forget we have a body.

Here's the secret—
are you ready?

That's right!

You **get up**
& shake
& wiggle
until you giggle.

Go ahead, try it! I can wait. ;)

Do you notice anything different with a freshly wiggled body?

Something about moving, bouncing around, and feeling your body go back and forth jumpstarts you into **Kairos** time, it puts you back into the here and now.

Like the ultimate reset button!

When you do it,
you're back to **choosing** how
you want to spend your time.

Special ability unlocked!
Wiggletastic Moves: level 2

So instead of feeling stuck watching videos for 4 hours, you can choose to just watch one or two...

and then invent a whole world in your notebook, or spend time on a walk exploring your neighborhood, looking at new buildings and plants.

Special ability unlocked!

Advanced Mindfulness

Not all time spent on technology is **Chronos** time, and sometimes Kairos time involves different kinds of technology—*like trees!*

Remember, technology isn't *all* bad!

But we need to remember to feed our bodies as much as we feed our minds.

So the next time we're feeling stuck, tired, or just out of our bodies and want to change it...

Remember there are many ways we can feed our bodies

not just with food

but with taking deep breaths

with fresh air

with movement

And with big hugs!

Outro

Technology affects all of us, sometimes in positive ways, but other times, not so much. We have to remember that sometimes when we look to technology, we're really looking for belonging or comfort, but we don't need technology for that. We can give that to each other by spending quality time with those we love.

So, here are some things you can do with your kids to get away from your devices for a bit and put yourself back in balance.

- Throw a ball.
- Have a dance party!
- Share a meal.
- Go on a walk.
- Play with a pet together.
- Talk and listen to each other—and don't bring up work or things they need to do!

find
more
kids
books
about

community, diversity, gender, autism, adoption, emotions, climate change, addiction, sexual abuse, suicide, and immigration.

akidsbookabout.com

share
your read*

*Tell somebody, post a photo, or give this book away to share what you care about.

@akidsbookabout